OOPS! ACCIDENTAL INVENTIONS

BUBBLE GUM

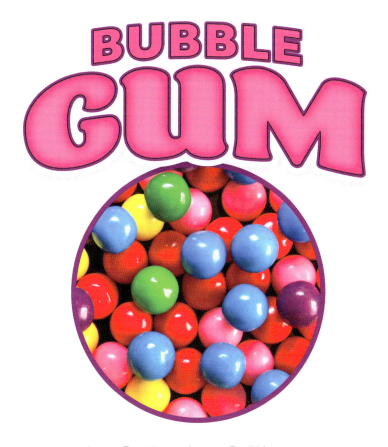

by Catherine C. Finan

Consultant: Beth Gambro
Reading Specialist, Yorkville, Illinois

Minneapolis, Minnesota

Teaching Tips

Before Reading

- Look at the cover of the book. Discuss the picture and the title.

- Ask readers to brainstorm a list of what they already know about bubble gum. What can they expect to see in this book?

- Go on a picture walk, looking through the pictures to discuss vocabulary and make predictions about the text.

During Reading

- Read for purpose. Encourage readers to think about bubble gum as they are reading.

- Ask readers to look for the details of the book. What happened to take gum from an accident to a favorite candy?

- If readers encounter an unknown word, ask them to look at the sounds in the word. Then, ask them to look at the rest of the page. Are there any clues to help them understand?

After Reading

- Encourage readers to pick a buddy and reread the book together.

- Ask readers to name two things that happened when bubble gum was being developed. Find the pages that tell about these things.

- Ask readers to write or draw something they learned about the creation of bubble gum.

Credits:

Cover and title page, © Daniel Zuckerkandel/Shutterstock; 3, © airdone/iStock; 5, © pkline/iStock; 7, © I_Lunaart/iStock; 9, © PeopleImages/iStock; 11, © Knulclunk/Wikimedia Creative Commons license 3.0; 12, © Studio KIWI/Shutterstock; 13, © Vinicius Tupinamba/Shutterstock; 15, © Prostock-Studio/iStock; 17, © PenelopeB/iStock; 19, © Wojciech Kozielczyk/iStock; 20, © Penny Hillcrest/Shutterstock; 21, © Africa Studio/Shutterstock; 22TL, © recep-bg/iStock; 22MR, © artorn/iStock; 22BL, © LeoPatrizi/iStock; 23TL, © karelnoppe/iStock; 23TM, © LightFieldStudios/iStock; 23TR, © erdikocak/iStock; 23BL, © NetPix/Shutterstock; and 23BR, © simonkr/iStock.

Library of Congress Cataloging-in-Publication Data

Names: Finan, Catherine C., 1972- author.
Title: Bubble gum / by Catherine C. Finan.
Description: Minneapolis, Minnesota : Bearport Publishing, [2023] | Series:
Oops! Accidental inventions | Includes bibliographical references and
 index.
Identifiers: LCCN 2022039492 (print) | LCCN 2022039493 (ebook) | ISBN
9798885093415 (library binding) | ISBN 9798885094634 (paperback) | ISBN
9798885095785 (ebook)
Subjects: LCSH: Bubble gum--Juvenile literature. | Chewing gum--Juvenile
literature.
Classification: LCC TX799 .F56 2023 (print) | LCC TX799 (ebook) | DDC
641.3/38--dc23/eng/20220831
LC record available at https://lccn.loc.gov/2022039492
LC ebook record available at https://lccn.loc.gov/2022039493

Copyright © 2023 Bearport Publishing Company. All rights reserved. No part of this publication may be reproduced in whole or in part, stored in any retrieval system, or transmitted in any form or by any means, electronic, mechanical, photocopying, recording, or otherwise, without written permission from the publisher.

For more information, write to Bearport Publishing, 5357 Penn Avenue South, Minneapolis, MN 55419.

Contents

A Chewy Accident 4

Bubble Gum Today 22

Glossary 23

Index 24

Read More 24

Learn More Online 24

About the Author 24

A Chewy Accident

Bubble gum is fun.

You can blow big bubbles.

Pop!

How did this **invention** happen?

The story of bubble gum starts with tree **sap**!

People chewed this sticky stuff thousands of years ago.

It was like gum.

In 1870, Thomas Adams started working with tree sap.

He tried to make a new kind of **rubber**.

But it did not work.

Then, Thomas remembered sap was fun to chew.

He made it into gum!

This chewing gum was a hit!

People loved it.

Other people started making gum, too.

In 1928, Walter Diemer made a new gum by **accident**.

Oops!

His gum was extra **stretchy** and sticky.

Say accident like
AK-si-duhnt

This new gum worked for blowing bubbles!

Walter made it pink.

Why?

That was the only color he had.

People loved Walter's bubble gum.

They had fun blowing bubbles.

Today, there are many yummy kinds of gum.

It all started with a few chewy accidents.

Bubble Gum Today

Most bubble gum is still pink today.

Many kinds of bubble gum have fruit flavors.

The biggest gum bubble ever was as wide as eight tennis balls.

Glossary

accident something that is not planned

invention something new that people have made

rubber a stretchy material

sap a liquid inside some plants

stretchy able to be pulled easily without breaking

Index

Adams, Thomas 8, 10
bubbles 4, 6, 16, 18, 22
chewing 4, 6, 10, 12, 20
Diemer, Walter 14, 16, 18
rubber 8
sap 6–8, 10

Read More

Cella, Clara. *Candy (Sweet Life).* Fremont, CA: Full Tilt Press, 2023.

Kids Ask: Who Invented Bubble Gum? (Active Minds: Kids Ask). Chicago: Sequoia Kids Media, 2021.

Learn More Online

1. Go to **www.factsurfer.com** or scan the QR code below.
2. Enter **"Bubble Gum"** into the search box.
3. Click on the cover of this book to see a list of websites.

About the Author

Catherine C. Finan is a writer living in northeast Pennsylvania. She once won a contest in fourth grade for blowing the biggest bubble.